FOREX TRADING FOR
BEGINNERS & DUMMIES

BY GIOVANNI RIGTERS

Table of Contents

Important Disclaimer

This book is presented solely for educational and entertainment purposes. The author is not offering it as legal, accounting, financial, investment, or other professional services advice. The content of this book is the sole expression and opinion of its author. It is not a recommendation to purchase or sell equity, stocks or securities of any of the companies or investments herein discussed. The author cannot guarantee the accuracy of the information contained herein. The author shall not be held liable for any physical, psychological, emotional, financial, or commercial damages, including, but not limited to, special, incidental, consequential or other damages. You are responsible for your own choices, actions, and results. Please consult with a competent tax and/or investment professional for investment and tax advice.

Introduction

You will discover what forex trading is, how to get started in forex trading, and how to make a trading plan. You will learn how to assess your risk and manage it appropriately in the trades you will conduct.

This book is going to teach you the do's and don'ts of forex, to help you avoid the most common mistakes traders make. Why not learn from experts who have already done things incorrectly? By learning what not to do, you have a leg up against anyone else who tries to enter the forex market without proper knowledge. The difference between profit and loss is always going to be your knowledge of how to invest in the forex market.

Plenty of information is needed to help you understand how the market moves the way it does, who moves the market, and how other investors conduct market analysis. Currencies are going to be explained based on the factors that drive them to move, as well as how to read a currency quote.

The forex market is like the stock market in some respects. You have technical analysis protocols that can help you trade on trends and certain popular patterns like support and resistance. You also have fundamental factors that drive the currencies to change.

Basic fundamental and technical analysis strategies will be discussed to help you plan and strategize for your entry into the forex market.

Chapter 1: What is Forex?

Forex is the trading of currencies across a foreign market. Forex is short for foreign exchange. This asset class exchanges one country's currency for another, which allows people to use it for a variety of things, but the most common is tourism.

Forex sets a standard rate for exchanging currencies, and this allows people to be protected from fluctuation risks. Seeing as this is a global industry, you have to deal with countries in their native currency. Back before the influx of the internet, currencies were allowed to just float around and fluctuate at will, until investors and banks took interest in it, and set a standard rate of exchange in which to back the currencies off of.

How to Get Started with Forex Trading

Getting started with forex trading requires you to gain knowledge, set up an account, have money to invest, and learn about the currency pairs you want to trade. You will need to build your dedication, resources, discipline, perseverance, decisiveness, and knowledge if you want to become a successful forex trader.

Gaining Information

Knowledge is key to your success. There are two questions every forex trader has to answer:

• Why do currencies change the way they do?

• How can you profit from that movement?

You are going to learn the answers to both these questions, as you read through this book. For now, to get started, you need to understand that knowledge is the powerful key to trading in the forex market. Without the knowledge of how to trade, how the market works, and the mistakes that can be made, you will not be able to make a profit.

You have already started on this first step of getting started in the forex market. You are learning.

As you gain knowledge, you will need to understand the economic, political and market dynamics. Only when you have this knowledge and understanding, will you be able to experiment with trading strategies, figure out various order positions, and improve your profit margin.

Before you trade with real money, you need to practice what you learn. The goal as you learn is to work towards a profit margin of 90% or higher. At first, you may see a profit margin below 50%, meaning significant losses. By setting up a paper money account, you can avoid real losses.

Set up an Account

Finding a broker is important, so you can set up your account for trading currencies. You want to set up an account that allows you to trade with paper money, as well as trading in real market conditions. Paper money accounts mean there is no risk to your capital until you are satisfied that you are ready to trade with the risk of losing that money.

Accounts will vary concerning what you need to set one up. The brokerage firm will need to verify your identity. You can enter your details online since this is where you will be trading currencies. Make sure all of your information is accurate, including your address, social security number, and personal banking information. The broker will ask for you to verify your information by sending a copy of your driver's license and a form to them.

After the form is received and processed, your account can be used for real money trades. While you wait for your account to be set up for real money trades, you will be able to access the paper money account. It only takes a username and password for paper money software.

Brokers require a specific amount of money to trade because of how the forex market works. There are small batches that some brokers will allow you to trade. A small batch is $1,000 per open order. It means if you wanted to invest in the EUR/USD you would need at least $1,000 to buy or sell the currency. Other brokers require a minimum of $10,000. Some brokers require $100,000 or $1 million. Until you have the money balance the broker requires, you will not be able to trade.

Get Money Prepared

Preparing the money for currency trading is about more than the minimum $1,000 or $10,000 most of the small investors are required to have per trade. If a broker requires $1,000 per trade, then you need to have at least $3,000 in your account. You wouldn't want to put all of your money in one basket, right? Trading is about diversifying, where you hedge your trades against other positions to ensure a profit at the end of the year.

If you only have $1,000 to invest and that trade goes wrong, you are no longer solvent enough to invest in the forex market.

Now, as you are learning about the forex market, is the time to figure out how much you need to open a real money account. Brokers require different starting capital, so when you learn how to find a broker—don't forget to learn what their starting capital requirement is.

Also, don't rush into getting the money prepared if it means tapping into a retirement account or investing money you don't have to spend. There is a lot for you to learn about the currency market before you will be ready to trade.

Currency Pairs to Trade

The forex market is all about trading currencies, thus it makes sense for you to know which currency pairs you should or want to trade. Part of getting started is assessing the risks of various currencies available to trade to determine how best to make money from the forex market. Not every currency used around the world is available for trade on the forex market. Smaller countries may not have enough currency volume to be traded. Brokers may also not offer anything other than the top major and minor currency pairs because it doesn't provide enough of a profit for them to offer the extremely minor currency pairs.

Dedication

Dedication is required to get started with forex trading. If you do not have the time and energy to spend on trading in the forex market, then you may make mistakes and lose your hard-earned money. A person who truly wants to invest for the profit found in forex is going to have the time and energy to learn about the market, how it works, and how to place a trade.

Resources

Resources go beyond the books, articles, and money you prepare to get started in the market. You also have to have the technology to get started. If you do not have a computer with an internet connection, it will be harder to invest in the forex market. Furthermore, the technology you have has to be able to support the trading platform you choose to use. A slow internet connection could time out before you know if a trade was placed. Since trades can happen in minutes, where you make a profit in 5 minutes, you want an internet service provider that can ensure you know what is happening in real-time.

Discipline

Discipline is both a financial and an emotional topic. Already, you know that you have a certain amount of funds to invest in the forex market. However, you also have the discipline to not lose that money all in one trade, in a couple of bad trades, or to get greedy about the profit you can make. It takes discipline to stick with a trading plan to ensure you earn the 90% profit margin that you are going for.

Emotions can affect your discipline. Emotions such as fear and happiness can cause mistakes. If you are too afraid to enter the market, you won't earn a profit. If a great trade makes you happy, it could also make you sloppy or make you ignore the risk management plan you have in place. Anger may make you try to recoup the losses you suffered, only to gain more losses versus a profit. Caution is a good emotion unless it leads to inaction. Overall, you need the discipline not to follow your emotions, which you will learn about in the chapter: Trading Psychology.

Decisiveness

Decisiveness is the power to make a trading plan and put it into action based on the knowledge you have of the currency pair you will trade. You have to be decisive to make a decision. This can also be rooted in psychological factors, as well as intellectual. Your intellect will tell you that you know something about a possible profitable trade, your emotions have to be reined in so you follow through with the action.

Perseverance

Having perseverance will help you get started in the forex market. It is about risk management versus opportunism requirements to trade. You have to determine your risk tolerance, persevere even if a mistake was made in your market assessment, and take advantage of opportunities that you spot in the market.

Foreign Exchange Market

This is a market that has to do with everything in the foreign exchange market. You can buy, speculate, sell, or even exchange currencies. This market is made up of banks and companies, brokers and investors, and much more. These firms and people make it possible to have a steady exchange rate in foreign currencies, to reduce the risk of fluctuation.

Forex provides a floor for speculation and processing of currencies, along with conversion and investment of currencies. It has a high rate of success and draws in many people from across the board.

There are many reasons why this market is desirable.

• Flexible Hours: This market is open for 24 hours Monday through Friday. It is only closed on the weekends. This means that someone who works a normal nine to five job, or someone enrolled in school, can still access the benefits of currency trading on their time off, without having to interrupt their daily routine.

• Large Industry: Forex is the largest industry in the world of finance, with several banks, and outlets to choose from, there is always a space for a new investor or trader in the market. With over four trillion dollars traded daily, billions of that was in currency and options trading.

• High Assets: Being one of the most impressive assets in the world, Forex has some high liquidity. That means that any assets you put into this process will be safer than anywhere else. There will always be money to be made in this industry

• High Leverage: The amount of leverage in this business is astounding. You can have a thousand dollars and trade it for a hundred thousand dollars' worth of currency. This is the best part of Forex trading. It gives you the power to become powerful. You will earn money without having to work extremely hard. You just have to learn a few things and let the leverage work itself out

With perks like that, it is impossible not to be intrigued by this amazing investment opportunity. The ability to make money so easily is worth every penny you put into it. Forex trading is simple, as long as you are willing to put in a little money and learn about exchange rates.

Being the biggest currency industry out there, there are always openings, so you don't have to worry about fighting for a spot. All you have to be willing to do is try to get in. A little bit of knowledge, and a whole lot of confidence, and you will be on your way.

Breaking down the market is pretty simple as well. It is not centrally located but is a global market that has so many different outlets it will make your head spin. The exchange rates are also not set with profit in mind, but standards and policies, which means they can't be changed at whim. This is a good thing because going in, you will know the basic exchange rate, and will be informed well in advance of any changes. This is unlike any other investment market where things can change in the blink of an eye.

A Forex broker may act as a market maker in his area as well if there are no major banks in play. It would be up to him (or her) to set the rate, and it would be in a personal best interest to set the exchange rates at a competitive rate to ensure that he or she has a lot of business in the near future, because most people prefer to deal with banks rather than straight brokers, as banks have stricter policies. However, human nature to get the best deal often wins out, bringing a broker who has chosen to be competitive more business, therefore ensuring the broker a profit.

The market also relies on a network of computers to run properly. These networks keep documentation of exchange rates around the world, and a person interested can look up and see where you would go to get the best exchange rate, or if there is any fluctuation in exchange rates. These computer networks are what made Forex possible because before the internet came around, exchange rates were very volatile. They would change from one hour to the next.

That is why Forex is such a good industry today. All the people in the network are working hard to keep the exchange rates fairly normal and never go back to the dark times of foreign exchange again.

History of Forex

Currency exchange goes way back into biblical times. As long as currency has existed, it has needed to be exchanged for one reason or another. This is because the world has never once agreed upon a currency as a standard. The reason for this is that money was made out of what was most common for the area. For example, in China, gold was the most common. However, in areas like Saudi Arabia, in ancient times, their crops and livestock were their currency.

However, when you went to the Temple once a year, (people traveled hundreds of miles on foot to go to the Temple) the tithe had to be of one currency. Either silver or gold, whatever was more available that year. This meant that they had to have someone to exchange their currencies. The people who exchanged these currencies were referred to Kollybistes, and they set up during Feast Time at the Temple once a year.

These people were ruthless, they often charged high exchange fees, and looked down upon the poor, often charging them higher fees than the rich. These men were not in it to help people find spirituality, but rather to help line their own pockets for the year. These people did not care about actually exchanging money, and often jacked the exchange rate up at whim, so they could have a larger profit, often stealing from the church, because that lowered the amount of money that people could give.

You have to realize that unlike now, there was no way that most of these people could have access to more currency than what they brought with them. They often brought a few small animals, or a small bag of local coins, or a small number of crops, whatever their tithe may have been, and walked with these for hundreds of miles. They often started their journey two to three months in advance to get to the Temple in time. They spent half a year traveling, and if they were lucky, they made it their alive without being accosted by robbers. So these people arrived with not much more than the clothes on their backs, and a few chickens or what have you, only to be told that they do not have enough currency to make a proper tithe, so they have to settle for less, and repent for their sins and hope that their measly tithe would cover all the sins they committed that year.

If you are familiar with the Christian Bible, you probably know the story of when Jesus flipped the table. (If you are not of the Christian religion, I do apologize, merely referring) Well in the story or parable if you will, Jesus came across the Temple during feast times. He saw these horrible Kollybistes taking advantage of people for their own profit, and was furious. He felt that any tithe available should be good enough for his Father, as people gave him the best they had. The Kollybistes were taking advantage of people's fear of Hell, and using it to line their pockets and fill their bellies. He was so angry that he flipped these large tables over in the courtyard, and screamed at these scam artists.

This was not the only time that currency trading was monopolized, however. The Byzantine Empire, in the fourth century, monopolized the trade of foreign currencies as well. The Emperor wanted to make as much profit as he possibly could off of foreign currency exchanges, as he wanted visitors to pay to visit his empire.

This created a major problem toward the end of this reign though, as many people decided to quit visiting the Byzantine empire. They wanted nothing to do with the monopolizing of tourism or currency exchange. The Emperor relied so much on visitors as an income source, that the empire fell, and could not be rebuilt.

Throughout time, currency exchange has been essential to people buying and selling goods, such as pottery, cloth, even food. The exchange rates in that time fluctuated so much that you never knew if you were getting a good deal or if you should wait an hour to see then. Currencies were not standardized until early modern times.

In the early eighteen hundreds, a well known Italian family by the last name of Medici decided that there needed to be a safer way to hold your money. They established the world's first bank, and all foreign exchange of currencies in the area had to be done there.

Along with deciding that there had to be a controlled environment for exchanging currencies, the Medici family also decided that there should be a standard currency backing all trade. Gold was chosen as the standard monetary backer. This continued for several years, until the beginning of world war one. People left the gold standard propelled by the onset of war, in hopes of gaining more control of international trade.

After the war, the pound sterling was very popular in the foreign exchange business. Cheaper than the gold backing, it was also less reliable. By this time, many different countries had jumped onto the forex bandwagon. Even the newly forming United States of America was in on it. England was pretty skeptical of the whole ordeal, however. In the beginning, they only had two exchange brokers. However, they too began to see the benefits of forex, and by 1922, Britain had jumped to seventeen bank-backed brokers and over forty firms with forex brokers.

After World War 2, the strict exchange rate of currency was ended, and currency exchanges were allowed to fluctuate again. This caused the market to crash and even caused it to close for about a year. However, one good thing did come out of this. Computers became the latest technology and replaced telephones for communication throughout the network.

After 1973, Forex was completely free-floating, meaning there were no controls on where they could trade, however, every trade was gold-backed. During this time, the United Nations had the highest rate of trade.

It is necessary to know the history to make sure that you truly understand the entire process. Otherwise, you will be out there floating blindly and not realizing what to look for. If you know what you are looking for, then you will be able to prevent any bad trades from ruining your bank account.

Chapter 2: Forex Trading on a Budget

If you just started in Forex trading, you must have been wondering whether you need to have a huge amount of money to start trading. So, is it possible for you to trade the Forex market with little money?

The fact is that you can trade with little money, but your profits will be limited. With a few tips though, you can successfully trade the markets without having to put down thousands of dollars on the line.

Educate Yourself

Before you can place your money on the line, you need to be educated about what to do before you jump in. Make sure you understand the basics of trading the Forex market and know whether your limited funds will give you profit.

Understand the risk management processes as well as other concepts before you put any money on the line. If you have put some money on the line, then you should withdraw part of it and put it in a course. It will give you concepts that you can use to turn your money regardless of how much you have.

Learning resources also introduce you to analysis techniques that give you an idea of what trade to place and when to do it.

Start Small

As a new trader, it is prudent that you start off with a small amount compared to putting all your money into the trade. Remember that you can't have the success you desire trading dollars when you cannot trade for pennies. To do this, you need to find the right broker that gives you a low limit trading account.

Patience is Key

Forex trading is all about having patience. When you start small, you might see it be frustrating and slow, but it keeps you disciplined. Make sure that you start small and grow your account step by step.

Profitable Forex investing takes time and patience. All those traders that you see making money on the market were novices on their first day, some were even worse than you. However, most of them started small and grew step by step to become the pro traders that they are right now.

Do It Regularly

As you refine the craft, make sure you make trading your habit. To do this, start investing regularly as you learn the ropes. Add funds to your account several times a week and you will see the account grow. The good thing is that you won't lose too much in any trade compared to putting up a lot of your money for trading.

How to Earn With Forex

There are a few steps to make money with Forex. Let us look at what you can do.

Grow Your Skills

When you have the right skill, you will make money with Forex trading. The Forex market is dynamic, and you have to keep up with the changes. As you trade, you get more and more knowledgeable about the things that happen in Forex trading. Take time to learn new techniques and engage with other traders to understand what they do to be successful.

The best way to learn about Forex trading is to make sure you look at the various reasons the market is moving in a specific direction. For instance, you might look at the analysis methods that are used by top traders and why they use them. You also need to understand what triggers make the prices to move in a given direction as opposed to another.

Learn to Perform Analysis

The analysis is all about using charts and other visual tools to come up with a decision. Forex trading gives you two major types of tools to use – fundamental and technical analysis.

Fundamental analysis focuses on events that will change the performance of a currency pair. On the other hand, technical analysis involves looking at price action and its effect on the market – including the trends, momentum, and reversal patterns.

We shall look at these analysis methods in detail later, but at the moment, just know that you have a chance to make more profit when you perform the right analysis before placing a trade.

Work with the Right Broker

A Forex broker makes it possible for you to execute transactions. This is just one of the major functions – a broker handles various other tasks that are vital to trading.

Before you can choose a broker, make sure that you understand what they offer in terms of features and look at the reviews that are left by previous traders. If you come across fraud alerts or issues with the withdrawing of funds, then look for another broker.

We shall explore different brokers and how to choose the best one for your needs in subsequent chapters.

So, making money on Forex is all about buying a currency pair at a low price, and then selling it off at a higher price to make profits. The profit, which represents your income, is the difference between the price you buy the price of buying and selling the currency pair. You pay the broker a commission from the trade called the spread.

If you believe that you don't have the capacity to place trades with your money, then you can use a feature given by the broker called the leverage. This is money that you follow from the broker to make your deposit higher.

Remember that the higher the deposit the more the risk.

Advantages of Trading Forex

When you get into Forex trading, you enjoy various benefits that come with the trades that you place.

Low Commission

The commission is the money that the broker makes on each trade that you place. Usually, when you trade in a different place, the broker takes a percentage of the money that you deposit to the account.

However, many brokers don't attach any fees on the trade, meaning that you can enjoy high-profit margins when you trade Forex.

Trading Flexibility

Forex gives you a lot of flexibility for both traders and investors. You don't have a limit to the amount you place on trade each day, which allows both smalltime traders as well as seasoned investors to make money.

Additionally, you don't have too many rules and regulations when it comes to Forex trading. This means you have the flexibility to work 24 hours without any disruption.

The flexible working hours make it possible for those people working day jobs to have some time to trade as well.

You have Complete Control over Your Trades

One of the top advantages of trading Forex is that you have total control when you place a trade. You don't have to run a trade that you are not comfortable with.

It is all upon you to decide when and how to place a trade without any obligation. You also decide the level of risk that you can take in every trade.

Demo Accounts Ideal for Practicing

As a rookie in the business, you need all the guidance and information to make it in the market. For you, a demo account is all you need to achieve the skills necessary to give you the push you need.

The demo account is a simulation of the way the live trading system works, and it gives you the practice you need.

When you use the demo account, you don't face any risk and it gives you an idea of whether the market is ideal for you or not. You also get to test, improve, and organize the new skills that might be beneficial when you start live trading.

Total Transparency in the Information You Get

The Forex exchange is a huge market and it operates 24 hours across different countries in various time zones. However big the market is, you get all the information you need to place trades. You will get information about the current forecast as well as the rates.

The information is real-time meaning that you get the information when it is displayed. This information is ideal for analysis so that you make deductions to the trend of the market.

Low Cost of Investment

Compared to other investments in the markets, Forex trading comes with a low cost of investment. The low cost of investment is due to the direct involvement by dealers which results in covering of risks; this means it doesn't need so much brokerage.

High Leverage

Compared to other forms of investments, Forex gives you the highest level of leverage than other investing markets. Even though you place a smaller amount of capital into the business, you have the capacity to win or lose big in the deals.

Wide Currency Pairs

When you enter the Forex market, you can trade in many currency pairs to your own advantage. With so many options to pick from, you get to enter a spot trade or opt for future agreement contracts.

You can choose the pair according to the budget or the type of risk that the pair comes with.

High Liquidity

The Forex market has the biggest number of players compared to other markets.

This leads to high liquidity that brings to the fore big players that fill large orders of the trade. It eliminates the manipulation of price, thus this promotes efficient pricing models.

High Volatility

In Forex, you can easily switch from one currency to another if you find it more profitable.

Remember that there is a high risk associated with investing capital in such a market, but with volatility, you end up with higher profit especially when you switch to a different currency that promises a good return.

This, in turn, gives you a higher advantage and increases profit.

Works for 24 Hours Each Day

The trading program operates 24 hours each day in a week which means you will always have a chance to trade no matter the situation. You can get from your day job and then handle any trades that you want during the evening.

You can take up Forex trading as a day job and you can work within the normal hours or your own preferred time. The good news is that you can still access the various tools and information that helps you to run the trades.

High Confidence Levels

When you make a profit, you get stimulated to run more trades. This creates a lot of goodwill. You can also get into the trade more thus make more money than ever.

The Disadvantages

Lack of Transparency

When you work with a brokerage, you tend to lose the transparency that needs to come automatically.

Make sure you work with a broker that follows all the rules that are involved in Forex trading.

While the market might not work under any regulations, which is a good thing, it might be constrained to the rules of the broker.

Price Determination

The platform goes through the price determination process, which is very complex. The outcome is that the rates are influenced by a host of multiple factors and reasons

For one, the global economy and politics are a huge influence in the rate of the currency and they end up creating uncertainty in the price of the exchanges.

You have to use your technical knowledge and other indicators to determine whether you are to face a loss or not.

Many Risk Factors

Various risk factors are involved in Forex Trading. For instance, there is high leverage that the results in high risks.

The uncertainty comes due to the price and the currency rate which, in turn, results in high profit or loss, so you have to be focused and knowledgeable about the market.

You are Fully Responsible for the Outcome

The Forex market allows you to interact with many investors that can help you run trades successfully. However, at the end of the day, you are fully responsible for the outcomes of the trades that you place.

This is the reason many newcomers end up quitting because of the losses that they suffer when entering the market with limited knowledge of the processes.

High Volatility

We have looked at high volatility under the advantages, but depending on how you experience it, this can turn out to be a disadvantage as well.

Changes in the economy usually turn out to be an issue on the process, thus it can be difficult for you as an investor to take a risk when investing the money.

When the changes are against you, it can lead to a huge loss to the investor especially when the market goes downhill.

Market Unpredictability

The market never shuts down; this means that you, as an investor, also have to be fully attentive, so that you don't miss out on any update. You have to stay updated at all times with the trends because these get updated each minute.

The market can change at any time, and thus you have to be conscious of what is happening in the market the whole day long. This means you have to be able to sit on the computer for hours waiting for the right trend.

Overconfidence

As time goes by, the trader experiences a set of winning trades that makes them overconfident. They fail to realize that they need to take caution with every trade, ending up with losing trades.

This overconfidence makes them lose their morale because they fail to realize that trading comes with losses as well.

The Need for Education

For you to enter the Forex trading market, you need to have enough knowledge of the subject. While you can learn on the job, it is advisable that you take a course or some classes to understand what it is all about.

Many people that have entered the market without any knowledge have had to contend with losses.

Many Scammers on the Loose

Another disadvantage of this trading method is that there are too many scammers ready to grab your loot. This is why you need to identify the best broker to work with that will not cheat you and that can guarantee you better returns.

Emotional Trading

Many traders end up trading emotionally, a factor that makes them lose more than they win. The biggest emotion in trading is fear, which is due to the uncertain trading environment that you are faced with.

Chapter 3: Risk Management

Risk management is about calculating the odds that your trade is going to be successful, according to Investopedia. Several factors can affect how currency prices change. You will learn about these economic, political, and investor factors later on. For now, just understand that you can control the risk you place your money in when you trade.

There are three things you need to understand about trading and risk that will help you protect yourself from high-risk situations. A high risk without any intellectual decision is gambling. You, as a speculator in the market, can strategize to lower your risk per trade, but only if you are willing to manage it properly.

Setting up an Order to Protect your Position

There are ways that you can set up an order to favor the expected outcome of that order. For example, the news indicates the USD will strengthen against the EUR, which means the currency price will go from 1.1426 to 1.10. But, what if the expected outcome did not happen? What if instead of the USD strengthening something unexpected happened? Perhaps, a terrorist attack occurred in the USA. Suddenly, the dollar weakened even further than it already was.

Know that when 9-11 occurred, the stock market and forex market took a hit. When the subprime mortgage crisis occurred the dollar significantly weakened against other currencies. The point is that while the market may indicate a certain outcome, it is up to you to ensure that you protect your position.

Liquidity Correlates to Risk

Liquidity is the amount of volume or number of sellers and buyers looking to trade at the current price. High liquidity can ensure a monumental currency price movement. Liquidity is going to vary for the currency pairs. Traders may be interested solely in the movements of the EUR/USD and not trading the AUD/USD, so the AUD/USD currency price quote is barely moving or only moving from one pip back to the original pip.

Not only is it about the market players, but you also have to have a broker liquidity that can make the trade. The trade cannot be filled if there is not enough liquidity to make it happen. Brokers work with banks, and as you know it all ties to the interbank system. If there is not enough liquidity a trade may not be placed, thus your trade may not be filled.

Risk per Trade

Your risk per trade is how much you are willing to lose if the market moves against your position. Many people determine that 2% of their trading capital is an acceptable loss for trades. If your trading account has $5,000 in it, with a 2% acceptable loss, then per trade you would not want to lose more than $100 to keep from losing 2% of your entire capital.

Let's take a look at pips again. A pip is 0.0001. If a 1 pip is 0.0001, and that is equal to $1 USD, then a change from 0.0001 to 0.0002, would be a change of 1 pip, which would be a profit of $1 USD for that trade. If the pip change from 0.0001 up to 0.0050, it would be a 50 pip move, or a profit of $50, if 1 pip is equal to $1.

One thing you need to realize about pips is that they do not always equal 1 in the currency you are trading. In fact, there is an equation to figure out your profit based on a trade you make, which has everything to do with lot sizes.

A lot size can be mini, which is usually $1,000. Lots are always in increments of 10s, meaning the next lot size is $10,000. A larger lot size would be $100,000 and up to $1 million.

So your risk per trade is a percentage of your capital, based on the lot size and the value of the pip. If we say $1 is 1 pip and you set up a trade, where you could lose 50 pips, then you have risked 1% of your trading capital or $50.

Leverage

The forex market works on leverage. Leverage is something every broker offers. You could put $1,000 down in a trade, but trade with an actual amount of $100,000. It is a leverage factor of 100:1, meaning a one pip loss is now equal to $10, so your risk of loss becomes $500, not $50. Some brokers will require you to use their leverage in the forex market, as a way around letting you invest smaller amounts in the forex market.

The good news—is you can limit your risk by having proper risk management. Risk management plans are based on your trading plan. Your trading plan helps you determine an entry position to take when opening a trade. Your risk management portion of that trade is the order type. The exit position or closing the trade is based on if your risk management order type was put into effect.

What are Order Types

An order type refers to how you enter or exit a trade. There are different types of orders that brokers offer. Some of these orders will not be provided by all brokers. A few of the orders are a little different, which is why a forex broker may not provide them.

Market Order

A market order allows you to enter at the best price currently available. You can buy or sell to open the position. If you wanted to buy a currency pair such as EUR/USD and the ask price was 1.1426, then the order would be filled at that same price. If you wanted to bid and the price was 1.1430, then the order would be filled at that price.

Limit Order

A limit order is going to limit how you buy or sell in the market. If the price was 1.1426, but you wanted to buy in at 1.1420, then you would enter a limit order. Your order would not be filled until the price hit 1.1420.

The idea is that you buy below the market price or sell above the market price.

Stop-Entry

A stop entry is like a limit entry you can set a certain price to buy or sell. The idea behind the stop-entry is to set it when you feel the price will continue to move in one direction versus either direction.

Stop-loss

This is definitely a risk management order, to put in place, when you have a trade-in effect. A stop loss is used to prevent losses. Perhaps you bought into the EUR/USD at 1.1426 expecting it to go up to 1.1430, but it went down to 1.1420. If you have a stop loss order that says close your position at 1.1422, then you lose 0.0004 pips, instead of 0.0006. A stop loss makes it possible for you to walk away from your computer, rather than sitting there monitoring what occurs. You can trade in the forex market and yet go to work without worries.

Trailing Stop

The trailing stop order is even better if the broker offers it. It is a type of stop loss, but it is more effective, should you wish to see if the market will return after a slight dip. For example, if you set a trailing stop loss at 1.1422, and the price rose from 1.1426 to 1.1428, then dipped back to 1.1423, you would close. The position would close because the trailing stop loss follows the profit. Your trailing stop would be set at 1.1424 because the price went up to 1.1428.

Let's look at a larger difference. You entered the market at 1.1426, the price rose by 20 pips. You have a trailing stop loss set at 20 pips difference. You said, close my position at 1.1406 if the price goes against your position. However, it went to 1.1446. The trailing stop then moves to 1.1426, so if the position turns back, you at least break even. If the price continues to 1.1466, you currently have a profit of 40 pips, the trailing stop loss goes to 1.1446. So, if the market drops from 1.1466 back to 1.1466, your position closes with at least a 20 pip profit. In other words, when the trailing stop price is hit, your position is closed with an immediate market order, so you retain some of the profit.

The advantage is that you get to retain some profit when the market moves in your favor, but if it moves against you—you have also limited your losses.

Good 'Till Cancelled

GTC or good 'till canceled allows an order to remain in place until you cancel it. In other words, if you want to buy at a market price, but before you can open the position, the market price changes, you can set a GTC. You enter the price you want and wait to see if the market price returns to that amount.

Good for the Day

GFD or good for the day is an order that you leave in place, until the end of the day. It will be eastern standard time, based on the New York forex market. At the end of the day, your broker will reject the order and not try to fill it the next day, unlike the GTC, which is there until you cancel it.

One Cancels the Other

OCO or once cancels the other is a mixture of two entry and/or two stop loss orders, (Babypips). This type of order is good if a currency pair has been in a rut, where the support and resistance lines are not broken for a fairly long trend. However, your research shows a possible break in the pattern, so you set up an entry point to make a profit on the breakout.

Perhaps, the market price is 1.1426 for the EUR/USD, and you feel the resistance level will be broken at 1.1450. With this type of order, you are making an if, then statement.

If the price 1.1450 is reached you buy, if the price goes below 1.1326, the sell order of that if, then the statement is canceled. The idea is that you want to buy in when the price is increasing or sell if the price is going below the support since this means you earn from the change in pips.

One Triggers the Other

This is also an if, then statement. However, it is the opposite of the OCO. With an OTO or one triggers the other order, you have an order which requires the parent order to be triggered. If the parent is triggered, then the profit-taking order is put in place. The profit taking order is set so you will not suffer a loss of money in the trade or of profit.

As you can see, there are plenty of ways to set up risk management plans on your orders to ensure you minimize the amount of money you lose, but gain the maximum profits.

Deciding the Risk

You have to decide how much risk you are willing to take on. Most people find 2% risk acceptable; however, you may like a higher risk-reward situation, where you are willing to risk more than 2% of your trading capital.

The risk is all about planning out your trade because it determines the profit or loss you make, as well as whether you have a profit overall or a loss for the year.

Chapter 4: Fundamental Analysis

To trade in the forex market successfully, one of the most important things you can learn is the most reliable way to spot a trade that is going to end up being reliably profitable from one that blows up in your face. This is where proper analysis comes in handy, whether technical or fundamental.

Fundamental analysis is easier to learn, though it is more time consuming to use properly, while technical analysis can be more difficult to wrap your mind around but can be done quite quickly once you get the hang of it. While both will help you to find the information you are looking for, they go about doing so in different ways; fundamental analysis concerns itself with looking at the big picture while technical analysis focuses on the price of a given currency at the moment to the exclusion of all else.

This divide when it comes to information means that fundamental analysis will always be useful when it comes to determining currencies that are currently undervalued based on current market forces. The information that is crucial to fundamental analysis is generated by external sources which means there won't always be new information available at all times. This chapter and the next are dedicated to fundamental and technical analysis, respectively.

Generally speaking, fundamental analysis allows you a likely glimpse at the future of the currency in question based on a variety of different variables such as publicized changes to the monetary policy that the countries you are interested in might affect.

The idea here is that with enough information you can then find currency pairs that are currently undervalued because the market hasn't yet had the time to catch up with the changes that have been made. Fundamental analysis is always made up of the same set of steps which are described in detail below.

Start by determining the baseline: When it comes to considering the fundamental aspects of a pair of currencies, the first thing that you are going to want to do is to determine a baseline from which those currencies tend to return to time and again compared to the other commonly traded currency pairs. This will allow you to determine when it is time to make a move as you will be able to easily pinpoint changes to the pair that are important enough to warrant further consideration.

To accurately determine the baseline, the first thing you will need to do is to look into any relevant macroeconomic policies that are currently affecting your currency of choice. You will also want to look into the available historical data as past behavior is one of the best indicators of future events. While this part of the process can certainly prove tedious, their important cannot be overstated.

After you have determined the historical precedent of the currency pair you are curious about, the next thing you will want to consider is the phase the currency is currently in and how likely it is going to remain in that phase for the foreseeable future. Every currency goes through phases regularly as part of the natural market cycle.

The first phase is known as the boom phase which can be easily identified by its low volatility and high liquidity. The opposite of this phase is known as the bust phase wherein volatility is extremely high, and liquidity is extremely low. There are also pre and post versions of both phases that can be used to determine how much time the phase in question has before it is on its way out. Determining the right phase is a key part of knowing when you are on the right track regarding a particular trading pair.

To determine the current major or minor phase, the easiest thing to do is to start by checking the current rates of defaults along with bank loans as well as the accumulated reserve levels of the currencies in question. If numbers are relatively low them a boom phase is likely to be on its way, if not already in full swing. If the current numbers have already overstayed their welcome, then you can be fairly confident that a post-boom phase is likely to start at any time.

Alternatively, if the numbers in question are higher than the baseline you have already established then you know that the currency in question is either due for a bust phase or is already experiencing it.

You can make money from either of the major phases as long as you are aware of them early on enough to turn a profit before things start to swing back in the opposite direction. Generally speaking, this means that the faster you can pinpoint what the next phase is going to be, the greater your dividends of any related trades will be.

Broaden your scope: After you have a general idea of the baseline for your favored currencies, as well as their current phases, the next thing you will need to do is look at the state of the global market as a whole to determine how it could affect your trading pair. To ensure this part of the process is as effective as possible you are going to need to look beyond the obvious signs that everyone can see to find the indicators that you know will surely make waves as soon as they make it into the public consciousness.

One of the best places to start looking for this information is in the technology sector as emerging technologies can turn entire economies around in a relatively short period of time.

Technological indicators are often a great way to take advantage of a boom phase by getting in on the ground floor as, once it starts, it is likely to continue for as long as it takes for the technology to be fully integrated into the mainstream.

Once it reaches the point of complete saturation then a bust phase is likely going to be on the horizon, and sooner rather than later. If you feel as though the countries responsible for the currencies in question are soon going to be in a post-boom or post-bust phase, then you are going to want to be very careful in any speculative market as the drop-off is sure to be coming and it is difficult to pinpoint exactly when.

If you know that a phase shift is coming, but you aren't quite sure when then it is a good idea to focus on smaller leverage amounts than during other phases as they are more likely to pay off in the short-term. At the same time, you are also going to want to keep any eye out for long-term.

positions that are likely to pay out if a phase shift does occur. On the other hand, if the phase you are in currently is just starting out, you can make trades that have a higher potential for risk as the time concerns aren't going to be nearly serious enough to warrant the additional caution.

Look to global currency policy: While regional concerns are often going to be able to provide you with an insight into some long-reaching changes a given currency might experience in the near future, you are also going to want to broaden your search, even more, to include relevant global policies as well.

While determining where you are going to start can be difficult at first, all you really need to do is to provide the same level of analysis that you used at the micro-level on a macro basis instead. The best place to start with this sort of thing is going to be with the interest rates of the major players including the Federal Reserve, the European Central Bank, the Bank of Japan, the Bank of England and any other banks that may affect the currencies you are considering trading.

You will also need to consider any relevant legal mandates or policy biases that are currently in play to make sure that you aren't blindsided by these sorts of things when the times actually comes to stop doing research and actually make a move. While certainly time-consuming, understanding every side of all the major issues will make it far easier to determine if certain currencies are flush with supply where the next emerging markets are likely to appear and what worldwide expectations are when it comes to future interest rate changes as well as market volatility.

Don't forget the past: Those who forget the past are doomed to repeat it and that goes double for forex traders. Once you have a solid grasp on the current events of the day, you are going to want to dig deeper and look for scenarios in the past that match what is currently going on today. This level of understanding will ultimately lead to a greater understanding of the current strength of your respective currencies while also giving you an opportunity to accurately determine the length of the current phase as well.

To ensure you can capitalize on your knowledge as effectively as possible, the ideal time to jump onto a new trade is going to be when one of the currency pairs is entering a post-boom phase while the other is entering the post-bust phase. This will ensure that the traditional credit channels are not exhausted completely, and you will thus have access to the maximum amount of allowable risk of any market state.

This level of risk is going to start dropping as soon as the market conditions hit an ideal state and will continue until the situation with the currencies is reversed so getting in and making a profit when the time is right is crucial to your long-term success.

Don't forget volatility: Keeping the current level of volatility in mind is crucial when it comes to ensuring that the investments you are making are actually going to pay off in a reasonable period of time. Luckily, Luckily, it is relatively easy to determine the current level of volatility in a given market, all you need to do is to look to that country's stock market.

The greater the level of stability the market in question is experiencing, the more confident those who are investing in it are going to remain when means the more stable the forex market is going to remain as well.

Additionally, it is important to keep in mind that, no matter what the current level of volatility may be, the market is never truly stable. As such, the best traders are those who prepare for the worst while at the same time hoping for the best. Generally speaking, the more robust a boom phase is, the lower the overall level of volatility is going to be.

Think outside the box on currency pairs: All of the information that you gather throughout the process should give you a decent idea regarding the current state of the currency pairs you are keeping tabs on. You should now have enough to be able to use this information to determine which pairs are going to be able to provide you with the most potential profit in not just the short-term but the long-term as well.

Specifically, you are going to want to keep an eye out for pairs that have complementary futures so that they will end up with the greatest gap between their two interest rates as possible.

Additionally, you are going to want to consider the gap between countries when it comes to overall output and unemployment rate. When looking into these differences you are also going to need to be aware of the fact that shortages can cause constraints to capacity or when the unemployment rate drops, both of which can lead to inflation as well.

This, in turn, leads to an increase in interest rates which leads to a general cooling of the country's economy. As such, these factors are extremely important when it comes to determining the overall disparity between the interest rates of specific countries in the near future.

Furthermore, you are going to want to keep tabs on the amount of debt that the countries in question are dealing with, as well as their reputation of repayment on the global market.

Specifically, you are going to want to look for a balanced capital to debt ratio as the healthier that this number is the stronger the national currency is going to be no matter what else is currently taking place. To determine this ratio, you will want to know how much capital each country currently has on hand as well as their position when it comes to other nations and their level of reserves and foreign investment.

Understand their relative trade strength: If you find a currency that is currently in the middle of a boom phase, the overall strength that its fundamentals show will determine how likely those who are holding it in various currency pairs are to hold or sell. The same also goes for currencies that boast an overly strong or overly weak interest rate when compared to other, similar currencies.

What this means is that when a given currency is in the earliest part of the boom phase you will be able to easily find a strong market for its related currency pairs which combine agreeable fundamentals and strong interest rates. While all of these factors are important, as a general rule a strong interest rate will always trump subpar fundamentals.

Watch out for market sentiment

While determining specifics in undervalued currencies is useful most of the time, sometimes the market simply doesn't behave in the way that it realistically should. In these cases, it is the market sentiment that has hijacked the price of the currency in question and learning how to stay on the lookout for its influence is guaranteed to save you from some seriously unprofitable trades in the long run.

Like many things in the forex market, this is easier said than done, however, which is why it is best to take the following suggestions related to reading market sentiment to heart if you ever hope to get a clear idea of how strong the momentum regarding a given currency truly is.

Choose the right trend: Each and every move that currency makes is ultimately based on a trend that started building hours, if not days before. As such, if you spend time trading with either the 15 or 60-minute chart then you may find yourself accidentally moving forward based on part of a larger trend that is ultimately going to end up moving in the opposite direction.

As such, to avoid such mistakes, you are going to want to start by identifying the trend in the daily chart and then working inward from there until you reach your target chart. This will allow you to more easily determine the breadth of a given chart and allow you to avoid trading based on anterior movement as well.

Find the right price movement: On the topic of price movement, depending on the pair you are trading in, you will likely come across profits that you might not otherwise bank by simply getting a feel for the way your favored currency pairs move on a regular basis. Getting a feel for price movement means understanding the speed at which the pair typically moves, in both directions, to ensure that you know the most effective time to strike.

When the movement is clearly headed in an upward direction with a quickness, only to slowly descend after the fact, time and again, then you can expect other traders to be steadily buying into the pair without taking the time to do all the relevant research. This, in turn, means you can expect the overall sentiment of the market to be bullish which means you can respond appropriately.

Similar information can also be determined based on the way the market responds when new relevant information, both positive and negative, comes to light. As an example, if there was just a round of positive economic news out of the United Kingdom but the positive change in the GBP and USD pair doesn't seem all that enthusiastic, then you can safely determine that the market is moving in a bearish direction when it comes to GBP/USD.

Watch your indicators of volume: While there are a wide variety of different indicators that measure volume, there are no better means for doing so than the Commitment of Traders Report which is released each and every Friday. This report clearly outlines the net of all the trades made, both long and short, for the week, for both commercial and private traders. This is a great place to start if you aren't sure what currencies to favor as this will show where most of the interest was for the proceeding week.

As previously noted, it is best to always trade on the trend which means that if there are more net longs overall you are going to want to buy and if there are more net shorts overall then you are going to want to sell.

When this is not the case is if the buy positions are already at extreme levels then you will want to sell or at least wait until things move in the other direction because there can be no more increase if everyone who is going to buy has already bought. Eventually, you will see a reversal in this case which means that if this is the case then you are better off trading in the medium term instead.

Look more closely at international trends: When you are first getting your start in the forex market you are likely going to be surprised at just how interconnected the world as a whole really is. While some of these connections are going to be obvious, other will certainly catch you off guard the first time you encounter them which means you will want to pay attention to the way news affects various currency pairs, even if you are not actually trading in them at the moment as you never know when that information might be useful again at a later date.

Chapter 5: What is Technical Analysis

The first strategy that we looked at when it comes to Forex trading is fundamental analysis. For many traders, that is the preferred method to go with. Fundamental analysis allows them to look at the currency, as well as the country, economy, and government behind that currency to determine if it is time to invest in a currency pair or not. It can work really well for a lot of traders, but another strategy that you may want to consider includes technical analysis of the currency.

Technical analysis is all about looking at what has occurred with currency in the past. You may look over the past week or look at a decade or more. This kind of analysis will have you take a look at a lot of different charts and graphs, and you may even have to look at some older newspaper articles and magazines to figure out why certain ups and downs occurred in the charts.

The point of doing all this is to get a good idea of all the trends and overall movements that occur with that currency. While this can work for a country that happens to stay pretty steady, there can be some issues that make it harder to work with this kind of analysis in the Forex market. For example, this kind of analysis is not able to make predictions about massive disasters or times of uncertainty in the market. Simply because a country hasn't experienced these in the past doesn't mean they won't work in the future.

Most traders who use technical analysis will combine it with some of the other fundamentals that we discussed to strengthen their knowledge and ensure that they can see things from more than one angle. Of course, technical analysis is done mostly from charts (you can see if your broker offers these as part of a package on their platform), and then you combine these with other research such as checking the news and other fundamentals to make the best decisions.

The charts that you will use are known as price charts, and their job is to show you the exchange rate of a currency over time. Depending on the timeframe that you want to look at, it is possible that you will see a lot of information on that chart. For example, if you pick out a chart that spans a decade, the chart is probably going to look more like a flat line over time. But if you zoom in on the chart a bit more and look at just one year, you will see that there is a lot more movement up and down.

The time frame that you rely on is going to be really important. This is because a Forex trader has to really consider the time frame that they want to trade with. You want to look for a few things such as the best time to make a move when a trend starts moving. To do that, you must look through some daily charts and make predictions about whether the trend you see will continue or reverse in the next few hours.

As a beginner, you will spend a lot of your time looking at the simple moving average. This average is going to calculate from a set of price points by adding them together and then dividing the outcome by the number of points that you choose. If you do go with this one, it is best to go with about 20 points for the most accuracy. As you progress, you may find that the weighted moving average is better for you because it is going to give some more weight to recent trades that have been able to impact the trend.

So, what information are you going to look for to be able to get out of these charts? First, you will look for support and resistance. Throughout the day, it is pretty normal for a currency pair to bounce a bit, going between a high and low level. The lower part is the support, and the higher point is the resistance. This is going to happen because traders are working to buy and then sell currency to take advantage of some of the pip changes that will occur.

When a particular currency pair hits one of the supports, you can buy into it. Then you wait until it gets back to, or close to the resistance, before selling. To make sure that you are effective with doing this, you will want to make sure that there are some protection orders to help you get out of the market if there are any unexpected changes.

This method can be nice because it is effective. Many other traders are doing the same thing. They all buy in at the same time, which causes the value of the currency to go up, and then they will sell at the same time because they see that the currency value is getting back to the resistance level. This will cause the value to go back down. It is a trend that keeps on happening because so many people enter the market and try to use this plan.

This doesn't make it a bad option. It basically just shows that it can be an effective one for you to try out. Just make sure that you are certain of the support and resistance levels along the way. And don't think that you have to get it at the exact support and exact resistant levels. Hitting that exact point is pretty much impossible. Just try to get as close as possible, and you will be able to make some good income from this kind of investment.

Another trend that you can look at is the breakout trend. These are the trends that will break out of the resistance and support curve, and often, they show up after a new event, or a piece of news is released. This is where you will want to bring in your knowledge of the economy so that you can determine when a breakout is going to occur. If you guess correctly, you can get into the market before the price goes up and sell when it reaches its top. Or you can get out of the market in time if the news is bad or brings up uncertainty before the market crashes and you lose out on all your money.

Many traders find that working with technical analysis can be a great option to help them earn a good amount of money in the Forex market. It does require looking at a lot of charts and graphs to see success.

But for those who can learn about the trends that occur with a specific currency, and who are willing to watch out for some big news items that may change the course of their currency pair away from its historical values, then technical analysis may be the right option for you.

Chapter 6: The Forex Broker

The Forex broker is the entity that connects the trader to the market. The broker gives you the chance to open an account, and this account is the one that you use to purchase currency pairs and hold them.

The broker makes all this possible for you. Before the advent of brokers, you had to invest a huge amount of money and create a special relationship with banks just to buy the currency.

The broker makes money by charging a commission when you make a trade. The change in the relationship when you trade a currency pair is called a pip. The broker charges you several pips before you trade.

So, whether you win or lose a trade, you have to pay a small amount of money to the broker.

The major task of a Forex broker is to give you easy access to the Forex trade market while he makes money.

You will come across many Forex brokers out there, some small, some big but all of them work in the same fashion. These brokers are regulated by bodies that are put in place by the different economies across the world.

Reasons why you need a Forex Broker

So, why do you need a Forex broker in the first place? Here are the reasons:

1.   Gives You access to Trading Platforms

The broker gives you unlimited access to reliable and legitimate trading platforms. Remember that the wrong platform makes it hard for you to make money in Forex, which is why it is vital that you work with the right broker to do this.

The wrong trading platform also eliminates the element of time wastage. This is why it is vital that you work with the right broker for this task. The right platform gives you all the access you need as well as tools to achieve the trades that you need.

To connect to the market, you need to make sure you work with a reputable broker. Some are scammers and you need to watch out for this.

We shall cover the trading platform later, as for now, we focus on the broker.

2.   Allows you to Take Advantage of Leverage

Leverage is the act of borrowing funds to place your trades. This makes it possible for newbies that don't have enough funds to place huge orders.

The right platform gives you a high ratio of leverage to use to supplement your capital. As much as leverage is good for you, it can also work against you, especially when the market is moving in the opposite direction than what you predicted. When this happens, you stand to lose a lot of money.

3.   Offer Various Tips

A good Forex broker will give you tips and knowledgeable articles so that you can gain the necessary skills to succeed. Some of the skills include helping you to access the tutorial that allows you to understand what is happening in the other markets. They also give you guides on how to trade successfully.

The right broker includes demo accounts in the platform. These accounts give you a simulation environment that gives the beginner a chance to know what it is like to trade live. The demo account also assists the seasoned trader to test out the various strategies before they start trading live.

The broker can also include posts on their blog that can point out some techniques that the beginner can use to advance. They also use blogs to give an insight into new concepts on the market.

Other brokers offer Forex tutorials which are both free and paid. Make sure you understand this concept and what you need to learn.

4.   Give You Low Fees

The right Forex broker will not take a lot of your money; instead, they take a small percentage that is nearly insignificant.

5.   Protect Your Interest

Reliable Forex brokers are under the regulation and rules of many institutions. These institutions help to manage the brokers as well as regulate the components of the market. Depending on the region, the Forex brokers are bound by rules that the institutions put in place.

The rules are meant to protect your interests in the market. These rules make sure that you have a reliable and transparent relationship with the broker.

When picking the right broker, you must pick one that is regulated by a known financial institution so that you can protect your interest. Brokers who aren't regulated tend to carry more risk compared to those that aren't regulated.

Choosing the Right Broker

Choosing the Forex broker is a huge task because all that you do in Forex trading depends on the barker. Here are a few aspects to look at when making the perfect choice.

1.   The Security

A good broker needs to provide you with a high level of security at all times. Remember, you are going to invest thousands of dollars in the system, and this means that the money you invest is transferred to an account that has been set up by the broker. You don't want to place all your savings in the hands of someone that isn't legit, do you?

The good thing is that you can easily check the credibility of a broker easily. All you need to do is to contact a regulatory body that will give you information on the broker.

Each country has a regulatory body that is capable of giving you this information. Before you put your money in the hands of the broker, make sure he is a member of the relevant regulatory body.

2.   The Transaction Costs

When you go into Forex trading, the main aim is to make a profit. You make a profit by deducting the various expenses form the selling price. Remember that the more the expense, the lower the profit from the trade. When trading in Forex, regardless of the currency pair that you trade-in, you will be faced with costs.

Every time you place a trade, you have to pay a commission or a spread that goes to the broker; this is why it is just natural that you go with a broker that gives you the cheapest rates.

At times, you might docide to go with a broker that charges more just because he is reliable.

Remember, it is all about making the balance between the security and low costs of the transaction.

Using a broker that offers competitive spreads helps your bottom-line greatly, and you don't want to sacrifice joining a broker that has poor execution just for the low costs.

When you choose a broker, you go up against different types of commission structures:

• Fixed Spread – this is a certain percentage of the actual price. They don't charge you a commission when you trade rather you pay a certain amount of pips that is charged on the price of the trade.

• Variable spread – this type of broker marks up the price of the trade, but the markup is determined by the market condition. This means that the amount you end up paying is variable and not fixed. High liquid times come with narrow spreads, while low liquid times come with a higher spread. Just like fixed spread brokers, variable spread brokers don't charge you a commission.

• Commission only – here, you won't pay a markup on the trade, but you pay a commission as per each lot.

3.   Easy Deposit and Withdrawal

Reliable brokers allow you to deposit the funds then withdraw them when you feel like without having to go through many processes.

Once you make your choice, the broker shouldn't make it hard for you to withdraw the profit citing some irrelevant reasons. The withdrawal process needs to be fast and efficient.

Some brokers force you to add money to the account before you can withdraw your proceeds, which shouldn't be the case at all.

4.   Offer the Right Trading Platform

Remember that all the activities that you undertake happen on the trading platform that the broker gives you. This means that if the platform doesn't work out for you, even if you have the right strategy, you end up losing out. This is why you must choose the right platform to make things work out.

When choosing the right broker, make sure he has the perfect platform that you can use.

We shall look at the different platforms later, but at the moment remember that the platform has a lot to contribute to the final results.

5.   Customer Service

There is no perfect broker on the market; it is all about giving you a service that makes sure you enjoy trading.

There are times when the platform might fail, and when this happens, you need to have direct contact with the representatives at all times.

6.   Currency Pairs Offered

There are many currency pairs that you can trade-in, but only a few get the attention that they deserve. When you choose a broker, make sure he provides the currency pairs that you are interested in.

7.   Financial Stability

The security and the financial stability of the broker need to give you the peace of mind you need to run trades successfully. When researching the broker, you must understand how strong the brokerage is. Some are small while others are big.

You will find this information from the regulatory body or the website of the broker. Remember that the safety of the account should be the primary concern and trading with a capable broker goes a long way in making sure you safeguard the account.

8.   Reputation

When you talk to a few established traders, you will realize that they usually recommend a few reputable brokers that you need to work with. This means that you have to go with a broker that has been on the market and has built a reputation for good trading.

You will notice a few new brokers that spring up each year, so you need to be careful when choosing the broker so that you don't turn out to be the guinea pig for the brokers.

These brokers also come with different ratings, with some having a high rating while others have a low one.

So, now that you know that the rating is vital, how do you go about determining how the rating? First, the regulation is a plus for any broker. As long as the broker is regulated, it means that they are highly rated in the Forex trading realms. You need to read about broker reviews so that you see what past and present customers are saying about the broker in question.

Another indication of the rating is the actual age of the company – how long has the broker been in the market. Brokers that have been on the market for more than 7 years deserve your business because it shows that they have mastered the art.

Features of a Good Trading Platform

Back in the 1990s, when traders realized how important trading platforms were to Forex trading, only a few companies had the tools to make them succeed in their trades. Since this time, companies have been working tirelessly to make sure that, as a trader, you have the best access to platforms.

Currently, the most successful platforms come with a host of tools and features that make the tools easy to use. One of the reasons why Forex trading is becoming popular is because of the high rate of growth of the industry, coupled with the limitless opportunities on the market. As a result, an unlimited number of traders have taken up the market and are now making sure that Forex trading becomes better and bigger.

Modern Forex trading relies a lot on using software and tools, which help to reduce the complicated trade activities into simple affairs. However, when choosing the right trading platform, you need to pay attention to various aspects that make these platforms ideal for the trade.

Simple to Use

The right platform should be simple to use. It needs to be simple enough for you as a new trader and advanced enough for seasoned users.

This means the platform should have the tools that make it easy for you to navigate and access all the vital actions that help you trade successfully.

Should Give Real-Time Information

The financial market is volatile and unpredictable. This means that you need to expect sudden changes in the direction. Due to this, the platform that you choose needs to have an option that gives you real-time data and prices.

To achieve maximum efficiency, the updates and changes need to come in real-time and fast, so that you make wise and timely decisions.

Not only this, but you need to access the information fast and in an easy manner. The platform should give you access to hourly, daily, and weekly reports at a convenient location.

Easy to Customize

The platform you choose needs to give you various customizing options so that it gives you all the functionality you need. The functionality should meet your specific needs and requirements as a trader.

To keep up with the latest technological advancements, the platform needs to give you access to the latest technologies in the market. The broker needs to be privy of the technological advancements in Forex trading and incorporate them into the platform all the time. This enhances the efficiency, mobility, and accuracy of the system. Additionally, it makes it convenient for the user to be able to safely log into the system.

Charting Software

Remember that you make your decisions based on charts that you interpret. You, therefore, need to choose a platform that gives you access to charts of all types.

Risk Management

Every business has risks, and this goes for Forex trading as well. You will come across different types of risks (covered in the next section) and you need to make sure you know how to handle them. The platform needs to give you a set of risk management tools that allow you to protect your profits while limiting the losses.

Speed and Stability

The platform needs to be built on top of a system that is stable and engineered for speed. Remember that the faster you execute your orders, the higher the probability of profitability. When the system is slow, you might end up losing on profitable trades just because the rate of reaction is slow.

In a normal market condition, when you hit the button to either buy or sell, you expect a speedy trade at a specific price. As a trader, you need to make sure the execution on the platform is fast and not full of errors. The order needs to be filled in seconds and not even minutes.

The speed might vary depending on the condition of the market. For instance, the speed of execution is slow during high volatility, but you need to understand because such situations are out of the control of the broker.

When the market is normal, you need to ask for the proper execution of trades from your broker. You can understand the speed of the platform during the demo phase.

Account Types

You need to choose a broker that gives you various account types to choose from. Each account comes with various features, which you need to understand so that you align the account with your strategy.

• Demo account – this refers to an account that simulates the live account. The account is usually loaded with virtual funds to allow you to practice trading. The practice account is ideal for rookies that are looking for a platform to try out their skills as they learn the ropes. It is also ideal for seasoned traders who are looking for a platform to practice new strategies.

• Live Micro Account – this is the smallest account that you can start with. It allows you to trade in micro increments and is ideal for rookies.

• Live Mini Account – this has become a popular account for many traders, especially novices. The increments are bigger than the ones in the live micro account.

• Live standard Lot – this is ideal for the traders who have a bigger account size. These come with better commissions and give you access to premium features that you can use to trade.

As you can see, the different accounts require you to have a certain level of funding capability as well as experience. As such, you must analyze your situation and choose what type of account is suited for you.

Promotions and Bonuses

As the years progress, the competition for your business from many brokers has grown, and at the moment, you can have over 100 brokers to choose from. Due to this, more and more brokers are offering incentives and bonuses when you sign up. Each broker gives you unique bonuses, which makes it good for you to check out the various categories of the bonuses before you take a step.

Here are some of the most common types of bonuses that you can come across:

•	Deposit bonus - a huge percentage of the brokers offer this deposit. It is ideal for new clients that deposit funds with a broker for the first time.

•	No deposit bonus – This bonus is made when you start trading. It might come after you reach a certain point in the trade, say, ten trades.

•	Forex rebates – under this, you get a rebate when you place certain types of trades. It makes more sense for seasoned traders than new traders.

Data Security

One of the security issues that are being grappled within the real world today is identity theft. Many people have lost their funds when their credit card information has been stolen online.

When you open an account especially online, you need to be sure that the information is in safe hands. Some of the information you will submit online includes your credit card information, passport, and much other sensitive information that shouldn't fall in bad hands.

It is vital that the broker's website is secure and uses encryption to make sure your data is always secure.

Automation of the Trading

Many traders don't have the time to sit on the computer and run the trades manually. When you have the time, you can do this, but if you have limited time on your hands, you must choose a broker that allows you to automate most of the tasks.

The major benefit of this program is that you can step away from the system and let the trade get executed on your behalf. It also eliminates the emotions that are a part of trading, making you benefit from the trades better than the way you trade when you are full of emotions.

When you decide to go this route, make sure the broker gives you the necessary infrastructure to achieve the automation.

Mobile Trading

The mobile age has made trading and other tasks easier because now you can do it without having to carry your laptop along. The good news is that you can access mobile trading platforms from most of your brokers. These brokers offer apps that you can use to trade directly using your smartphone. This makes everything convenient, and you can trade while on the go.

Typically, you get to access the various functions of the platform from your mobile platform. You get to open and close positions, manage any open positions, and set stop/limit orders as well as monitor charts. The only difference is that the interface might be smaller than when you do it on the computer.

Managed Accounts

For those traders that don't have time to place and monitor trades on their own, then the concept of managed trades is ideal. Such types of traders don't have the time to learn the ropes, and therefore, opt to entrust the entire operation to the broker.

When you decide to go this route, you need to open a managed account with the broker so that he manages everything on your behalf. With the account, you maintain proper control over the whole process, but you give the manager the capacity to trade on your behalf. The whole process depends on an agreement that you sign with the manager.

However, you need to have a huge capital base, usually of 20,000 USD or more.

Payment Options

Before you can start trading, you will have to deposit some money with the Forex broker. The broker needs to provide you with various methods of depositing money into the account so that you can place trades. There are many ways to deposit the money in the account, including credit cards, payment processors, and wire transfer.

Whatever the method, you need to understand that for the trade to work, you need to choose the best method to use that is suitable for you.

You shouldn't just assume that the broker has the method you desire without checking out their FAQs. Additionally, the broker will give you a limit as to the amount you can deposit using each method that he has placed down. For example, a broker might allow you to deposit a maximum of $400 using PayPal, but allow you to deposit more than $2,000 with a credit card.

You should look at each method and the maximum level you can deposit. Additionally, there are various regulations within countries that determine how much you can deposit and withdraw.

While some brokers allow certain methods to use for depositing, they don't allow you to withdraw using other methods.

Tools

As a rookie on the market, you need to access resources that can help you run the trades. You need to have access to webinars, books, and videos that guide you on how to use the platform. Others teach you about technical analysis as well as calculators.

Most of the tools are free of charge and they assist you in making valuable decisions. Knowing what type of information you need from the broker helps you choose what type of broker you need.

Other Fees

When choosing the broker, you need to look at the various fees that the broker comes up with. Some will charge deposit and withdrawal fees, wire fees as well as account transfer fees. Make sure you are aware of these fees before you join a platform.

Chapter 7: Things to Consider When Trading Forex

It is not true that to invest in forex you have to have a lot of money. It is true that with equal choices a successful trade makes it proportionate to the money invested. The really important thing is that, with whatever sum you start, the currency exchange can give you earning opportunities. It all depends on how you invest.

It is not an easy thing, as long as it is said, and it takes time and attention. There is only one way to earn from the forex market: sell your currencies at a higher price than the one you bought them. In short, to trade in currencies and get a profit, one must know how to choose. Here are 7 things to keep in mind.

1. Plan Your Trade

The first advice that we can give you about financial investments, is about the planning of investments, or understanding what are the best actions to buy and diversify your portfolio.

Even if you have never experienced this chain of events first hand, it's not a problem. Sooner or later you have to learn.

In order to better diversify your currency portfolio and understand where to invest, we recommend opening a demo account.

The demo account allows you not only to plan investments but also to:

• Carefully analyze the currency pair in which you want to invest;

• Plan your investment strategies;

• Familiarize yourself with the platform;

• Get familiar with the market.

If you decide to buy currencies unconsciously and then open a real account and invest without the right measure, then prepare to say goodbye to your immense capital.

Of course, this is not the most appropriate and wise way to invest.

2. Draw the investment plan you just made

To quote W. Edwards Deming, world-renowned essayist, and quality, management consultant:

"If you cannot describe the process of what you're doing, you do not know what you're doing."

As for everything that requires a certain discipline, it is important to outline its trading strategy: in this way, it will be easier to articulate it. Once your strategy is written, look at it to make sure it meets your long-term investment goals.

Writing and schematizing your strategy will give you a firm base to start again in times of chaos and will make you avoid making important trading decisions dictated by emotionality.

It offers you a clear outline to review and change if with time and experience you will notice defects or if you change your investment goals.

If you are a professional trader, having a written strategy in black and white will help you better understand the investment process.

3. Learn the difference between investing and speculating

Understanding the difference between a trader and a speculator is very important. You need to know how to "use" the difference if you want to make the most out of your investments.

Before buying currencies you have to evaluate:

- what do you want to get from the markets;

- what is your personal level of risk tolerance;

- if you are investing;

- if your goal is to speculate on the markets;

- the time you have available to spend on investments.

If you want to get the maximum profit in a tight time, then you must have a considerable minimum time to devote to the study of markets and financial instruments. So you must understand the difference between speculator and investor.

What does a speculator do?

The speculator is that trader who buys and sells shares to make a profit in the short term; in this case, we are talking about very narrow trade times ranging from a few minutes to a few weeks.

We do not talk about years or months.

They only take advantage of the price difference between the value of the sale and purchase of the deal.

The speculator's characteristic is that it is not interested in dividends distributed by listed companies.

What does an investor do?

Contrary to the previous one, the investor also defined as a long-term investor invests his capital by providing liquidity to the currency pair.

In this case, the trader will buy the so-called "lots" of a given currency. What is the goal of a trader? Keep the currency in his wallet for a longer period of time and make them profit!

Very important in this case is to understand what kind of player you are. Pay close attention to this step as this is essential in making money in the forex market. Most of the trader's operating strategies are based on fundamental analysis that is very different from those of a short-term gambler or speculator.

4. Understand the importance of timing (and the impossibility of getting it right)

Very important is to understand when is the right time to buy and sell currencies.

In this case, the timing is an indispensable part to identify the currency pairs to be bought.

If the correct price levels are not identified, there could very well be the risk of entering the market at a risky point.

This could be unfavorable and does not allow us to accurately quantify the transaction's risk-return ratio.

5. Learn your strength and weaknesses

Does your investment strategy follow your idea of how investments depreciate or appreciate? If so, how do you exploit your knowledge?

This question refers to your actual knowledge of the market. Ask yourself:

"What makes me smarter than the market? What is my competitive advantage?"

You may have special knowledge of the industry or have access to a study that few others know.

Or, you could get your own opinion by exploiting some market anomalies, as happens in the strategies for the purchase of securities with a low price/value ratio.

Once you have decided what your competitive advantage is, you need to decide how you can use it profitably to develop a trading plan.

Your investment plan should include rules for both purchase orders and sales orders. Also, keep in mind that competitive advantage could lose its profitability and its effectiveness if other investors will begin to adopt your own investment strategy.

Or, you can be convinced that markets are totally efficient, which means that no investor will ever have a real competitive advantage.

In this case, it is better to focus on minimizing commissions and transaction costs by investing in passive instruments such as futures.

6. Is your strategy versatile?

There is an old way of saying on Wall Street:

"The market can remain irrational longer than you can remain solvent."

Successful investors know where their investment performance comes from and are able to explain the strengths and weaknesses of their strategy.

As trends and economic issues change, many investment strategies have periods of great performance followed by periods of poor performance.

Having a good understanding of the weaknesses of your investment strategy is essential for maintaining confidence in the market and investing with conviction, even if the strategy has been, for the time being, "out of fashion".

7. Understand that a good strategy can be measured

It is difficult to improve or fully understand something that cannot be measured.

For this reason, you should always have a benchmark to measure the effectiveness of the investment strategy you are using.

This benchmark must be consistent with investment objectives, which in turn must tune into your strategy.

There are two types: the relative benchmark and the absolute benchmark. An example of a relative benchmark could be the EURUSD pair. An example of an absolute benchmark could be a performance target.

Even if it is a time-consuming process, it is important to consider the amount of risk you are taking with respect to the investment benchmark. This can be done by recording the volatility of portfolio returns and comparing it with the volatility of benchmark returns over certain time periods.

Chapter 8: Great Strategies for First Time Traders in Forex

The plan that you decide to go with is going to be completely personal. You need to decide which currencies you like to work with, how much risk you are willing to take, and how much time you have to devote to this process.

But as a beginner, there are some strategies that you can work with that can help you get used to the Forex market and can make your understanding of individual trades grow. As time goes on, you will start to experiment on the things you have learned, and you can adapt your decisions to what you know now. For now, we are going to take a look at some of the different trading strategies that you can try out to help you get started.

The first strategy that you can try out as a beginner to make the trading easier includes:

1.   Start out with a limit order. The reason you want to do this is to ensure that you purchase at a set price and you don't focus on the market price. The market price will often move up and down while the order is active, so it is better to work on the set price to keep things easier.

2.   Decide the possible gain that you want to get based on the pips.

3.   Decide what you would like the stop loss to be at to protect your risk.

4.   Exit the position right when you start to gain the profit that you aimed for, or when you hit the stop loss point that you decided on earlier. Never fall prey to the temptation to stick around and see if it is possible to make more if a currency pair bounces back. This gets you into a bad habit of sticking around for too long, and you can end up losing too much money in the process.

Now that we have a basic trading schedule down, it is time to take a look at some methods that you can go on that will help you to reduce your risks while also helping you to make a profit. This time, this is not so much a step-by-step guide like before, but more of three choices that you can make when you set up a new trade. You can either use them individually on their own, or in a combination together to get even better results. The three choices that you can make for your trades include:

1.   A stop-loss order: This is when you will decide what you will do if the worst-case scenario occurs. It is either the low or the high where you will reach a loss, and it is going to represent the maximum amount of money or capital that you are willing to take on a trade.

2.   A trailing stop loss: This is often a better choice for a beginner trader to go with. This is because it will follow the price and then will represent a certain

number of pips off that current price. If the market does end up turning, this option allows the position to close, but if it continues on the trend of going up, you can continue to make a profit until you reach your closing order later on.

3. A take profit: This is an order that will remove the profit that you gain during a trade while continuing with your position.

The next thing that we are going to take a look at is a good trading strategy that you might like when you want to work with analysis before making any trading decisions. Some of the steps that you will do to help you with technical and fundamental analysis at the same time include:

•   Look at how the economic situation is doing throughout the world. You may look at some of the major players in the market, but you want to first get an overview of how the economy is doing for everyone.

•   Now, it is time to narrow your scope to the specific currency pair that you would like to trade in. You can look for information, sometimes, through a news item or a report that will pertain to your chosen currency pair. Any news that will affect the movement of your pair is something that you should pay attention to.

• Look at some graphs to help you figure out what the resistance and the support for that currency pair will be at.

• In addition to coming up with where the resistance and support are for that pair, you should also look at whether there are any indicators for breakouts occurring.

• If you can look at a currency pair and find three different indicators that suggest that it is time to trade at a specific currency, then you know it is a safe and profitable one to go with. Once you find this, then it is time to set up the order.

The next plan that we will take a look at is an overall plan that can help a new trader go through all of their charts or all of the charts that you can get ahold of, and how to use the simple movement of resistance and support to your advantage. Some of the steps that you can take to utilize all those charts, starting when you sit down at your computer to the end of the trade will include the following:

1.   Take a close look at the index of the currency. You can use it to identify a currency pair that is showing good movement. If a currency pair is showing some good movement, it is worth your time to invest in it.

2.   Look at the charts for the pair that you want to trade in, making sure that the charts look at different time frames. Consider looking over the current week,

one month, three months, six months, and a year. You want to take special care to look for any patterns that occur across these time frames, especially ones that might have some impact on what is happening to the currency pair right now.

3. Look at the daily chart to help you get a good idea of whether you should sell or buy a currency. Move down to the four-hour chart and check to see whether the indicators stay the same.

4.   Then move to the hourly chart. This is the chart that you need to look at to find the resistance and support. If you can find these lines, then pay attention to all the intervals of ten minutes to see if these lines change at all.

5.   Once you know the best interval for buy or sell because you see that the resistance and support levels are hit, then it is time to make your position.

6. Set the positions and orders. You can exit out of your position when the movement has traveled down in the opposite direction. When the trade enters the support when you start with the resistance or the resistance if you start with the support, it is time to end the trade.

7. You can then repeat this with the next interval When you continue to do this, you will find yourself hitting the pip target regularly, and it won't seem too hard either.

Now, we are going to move on to the last strategy for the Forex market. This one is going to allow the beginner to make broad use of all the available information that is there for you. The steps that you need to take to make this one happens for your trade include:

1.   Choose the currency pairs that you want to work with according to several factors like which window of time you wish to trade in, which ones have the most risks, and which will show the best movement at the time.

2.   Look at your chosen sources for your fundamental analysis. You will want to use this to help you get a clear picture of what is going on in the countries of those currency pairs and how that may affect the currency while you trade.

3.   You can also look for indicators or the strength of a currency. You can always look at whether it is currently being under or overbought.

4.   Watch to see if there are any directional changes in the currency. This can sometimes happen when a market first opens because traders may make some changes at that time.

5.   Use a potential trend reversal as a basis and then look at both the hour chart and the fifteen-minute chart, to find out more information about this trend and whether it will actually take place,

6.   Decide whether you want to trade against or with this new long-term trend. This will depend on where the trend is going and the goals that you have in place.

7.   At this point, you will want to take a look at a currency matrix to see how those currencies are actually doing. This will tell you which currency out of the two will drive the movement that you are anticipating, and how much trade is going on at the moment between those currencies. When you figure out which of the two is the most dominant currency, you can look to see how it behaves with other currencies and then use this information to figure out whether the movement is risky or solid.

8.   Set your trade up so that it has a stop loss, remembering all of the data that you have already gathered. The more chances there are that a trend will change quickly, the riskier the position can be and the tighter you should set the stop loss position.

These are a few of the different strategies that you can use when it comes to working with the Forex market. Each of the trades that you decide to do will need some kind of strategy behind them to ensure that you are making smart decisions and won't be surprised later on because you stayed in the market too long or you went in without any idea of what you were doing. Make sure to follow one of these strategies or use fundamental or technical analysis (or even a combination of the two), to make your trading easier.

Thank You

I would like to thank you from the bottom of my heart for coming along with me on this savings journey. There are many books out there, but you decided to give this one a chance.

If you expand your knowledge by reading this book, then I need your help!

Please take a moment to leave an honest review of this book.

 This feedback gives me a better understanding of the kinds of books and topics readers like yourself want to know more about.

It also gives my book more visibility to potential new readers.

Leaving a review takes less than one minute and is much appreciated.

Other Titles by Giovanni Rigters

Stock Market Investing: 25 Tips for Beginners

If you enjoyed 50 Tips on Saving Money, you will want to read Stock Market Investing: 25 Tips for Beginners.

In this book, we delve into the dos and don'ts of investing. This is a must-read if you ever thought about investing.

Smart Investors Create Wealth

It's never too early to start your journey towards accumulating wealth. No one wants to work for the rest of their life.

I will show you what wealthy people have known for centuries on how to not only create wealth but also maintain it so you can pass it down.

Printed in the USA
CPSIA information can be obtained
at www.ICGtesting.com
LVHW011919270624
784184LV00006B/244